Paranormal Is My Normal

By Robin C. Mueller

Paranormal is My Normal

By Robin Mueller

Published by Book Web Publishing, LTD
Book Web Minis
All rights reserved
Copyright 2018

Cover photography attribution to Thorn Explains It All

ISBN-13: 978-1-941882-23-8

*Edited and Researched by Donna Paltrowitz, BS, MS,
Certified Reading and Education Specialist, Author*

*Photography, Graphic Design, and Research
by Dr. Jeri Fink, Author, Family Therapist*

Read cutting-edge Book Web Minis

Why Paranormal Is My Normal

Join me on a path that will open you to peace, love, and healing.

Other dimensions exist. This book will show you a path that I have known since early childhood. It will expand your mind so you can embrace "Inside the Light."

At an early age I gained entrance Inside the Light. I followed that path to a place where I found guidance throughout my life from the energy beings that exist there. Death is not the end but a new beginning. This knowledge changed my life forever.

Let me light your way so you can see beyond what your physical senses perceive. You are not alone.

A Gallup survey found three out of every four Americans believe in some form of paranormal phenomenon. A United Kingdom study showed half of all the people in London believe in ghosts. According to Pew Research Center, 72% believe in heaven – a place "where people who have led good lives are eternally rewarded."

Why me?

My natural ability to connect with the non-physical world enables me to relay compassionate messages, insights, and higher spiritual perspective from Inside the Light. I continue to gain a greater understanding and explore the connections between life and life-after-death.

I hold a BA in English Literature with a Minor in Psychology, and a Certification in Paralegal Studies. I'm a Certified Reiki Master and Energy Medicine Practitioner. My services include: Spirit's True Voice - Spirit Connection; Beyond Tarot; Light Board – A Soul's Picture; and The Akashic Records. My seminars include: Manifesting with Light; Teach Them How to Find Us and Workings of the Sacred Soul. I work privately with individuals, small groups, community groups, and in large group settings. I am also available to help fundraising for non-profits and charitable organizations.

For more than 20 years, I have been in private practice to assist others to transform the health of their mind, body, and spirit into more joyful and inspired lives.

Why Book Web Publishing?

Donna Paltrowitz and Dr. Jeri Fink are authors, journalists, editors, and photographers who work with leading professionals and expert practitioners to share their voices. Book Web Publishing produces original mini books in e-book and print formats. If you're interested in doing a mini book with us, check out our website, www.bookwebminis.com and contact us.

Donna Paltrowitz began her career as a NYC teacher and licensed reading specialist determined to teach children to enjoy reading. Her path evolved into developing, editing, and authoring more than 100 published children's books, adult books, computer books, magazine articles, and educational software programs. Her varied interests, from property management, positive psychology, and the spirit world are seen throughout her work.

Dr. Jeri Fink is an author, photographer, and family therapist/clinical social worker. She has written over 30 nonfiction and fiction books for adults and children. Her articles and blogs appear on and offline, including topics from the paranormal to the everyday. Her *Broken Series,* seven thrillers about psychopaths that live next door, are Amazon bestsellers. In *Book Web Minis* she explores cutting-edge nonfiction and fiction that confirms the power of positive meaning.

Paranormal is My Normal

Robin C. Mueller

CONTENTS

1 PARANORMAL IS MY NORMAL

Our path begins here.

Imagine walking through lush, green woods where every turn is beautiful. Most of it is real – you can touch leaves with your fingers, smell the woods with your nose, and feel the rough path beneath your feet. There's a magic in the air, dreamlike, enchanting, and invigorating. You can't measure it; you might not even be able to describe it in words. But you know it's there.

Welcome to Paranormal Is My Normal.

As an Intuitive Medium, Healer, and Guide, I've been deeply connected to the world of spirits all my life. I focus on offering a safe place for people who are searching to enrich their lives through universal healing energies. Understanding yourself and deeper, often forgotten spiritual bonds empowers you to transform mind, body, and soul into joy and inspiration.

I call this book "Paranormal Is My Normal" because I go beyond what science and the senses can measure.

I was 6 years old when I encountered my first spirit. I thought it was perfectly normal. After all, Mrs. Ryan was a neighbor.

Mrs. Ryan lived next door to me in the Bronx where I grew up. She was a youthful, active mother of two young boys. I sensed something was not right when I saw her two children sitting on their front stoop in black suits and ties. I can still remember the sadness I felt watching them. Years later I realized that they were waiting for the car that would follow a large black hearse with a mahogany coffin in the back. On the way to the cemetery, Mrs. Ryan had made a final pass down the street where she once lived.

The kids, not knowing any better, began to tell stories. "Murder," one boy screamed at me. "Mrs. Ryan was murdered!"

"Someone chopped off her head," another boy shouted, laughing as I ran away.

I hid behind a tree and pressed my hands over my ears. I wanted to drown out the voices. As hard as I tried, all I could do was pick up the images from *their* words. My imagination was triggered, filled with Mrs. Ryan and thoughts of how she died.

I was terrified.

That night when I went to bed, trembling. I lay alone in the dark, haunted by the image of Mrs. Ryan's severed head.

I was frozen with fear.

Slowly an image emerged from a circle of light.

As the image approached me, I saw it was Mrs. Ryan. She had a halo of blue light around her. She came closer and the light turned to brilliant white.

Mrs. Ryan spoke, more inside my head than my ears. "Don't be afraid, Robin. No one murdered me or cut off my head. An angel helped me come so I could ease your fear."

I stopped shaking.

"But you're alive!" I cried. "You look so beautiful." Mrs. Ryan was clothed in bright light with her long red hair cascading down her shoulders.

"There's nothing to be afraid of."

Suddenly, the fear fell away, replaced by inner peace.

Mrs. Ryan hugged me although I didn't exactly feel her touch on my skin. "It's a beautiful place. I'll be looking over my boys for their whole lives."

The Angel sent a bright blue light from her hand into my heart. I fell asleep instantly.

When I woke the next morning I wasn't scared of what the boys had said. I went to my mother and told her that Mrs. Ryan was okay and hadn't been murdered.

I knew then that there are spirits around all of us. With our busy lives, constant stress, demands from family, friends, and work, we don't have time to stop and be mindful of their presence. It doesn't mean they're not there – only that you don't see them right now. But like Mrs. Ryan watching over her boys, spirits watch over you, too.

We are not alone.

2 MINDSETS

"Paranormal Is My Normal" is because I move beyond the traditional mindsets into a different energy.

A mindset is how you view the world. It includes ideas, attitudes, and behaviors that keep your life on track.

There are three kinds of mindsets – *fixed, growth,* and *hybrid.* I have all of them – you might too. Life is a combination of mindsets, brought in when they're needed. Think of it this way. You don't need to have a political mindset when you're shopping for vegetables. You may use a health mindset to choose exactly what to buy at the supermarket. Will it be cake or cauliflower? How about chocolate chip cookies or grapes? You may use your skeptical mindset to shield yourself from advertisements of unhealthy foods. Perhaps you'll use an inflexible mindset to buy the same things every week, whether good or bad.

If I remained in one mindset I would have followed my early training as a certified paralegal. I never would have gone down this path or written this book.

Let's look deeper.

A *fixed mindset* is when you stick to already established beliefs. Change may be awkward or uncomfortable. You believe things are hard-and-fast – the basics, like intelligence and imagination, are set in stone. People or groups with a fixed mindset avoid going against the norm.

We all know people with fixed mindsets. Think about the following people. Do they sound like you or someone you know?

A good friend is great fun to be with but won't try anything new. Meeting her for lunch or dinner is always at the same restaurant. Her reasoning is that the "usual spot" is so good, why take the chance of going someplace that's worse?

A neighbor insists on keeping his old, crumbling wood fence? When a contractor suggests clean, easy care, long lasting PVC fencing he won't consider it. "I always had wood fences," he shrugs. "Why change?"

Perhaps an employee hates his new boss. "The new guy is always changing things," he complains. "Why bother when everything already works just fine?"

Do you know people like that? Maybe it's you? People with fixed mindsets always ask the same question:

Why fix it if it's not broken?

A *growth mindset* is different. It means moving outside the box to try different things, ways, and ideas. Growth mindsets challenge fixed mindsets. You may be right or wrong, but at least you gave it a chance. It means trying a different restaurant, checking out another fence, or working with the new boss's changes.

It can also be a skeptic who receives a message from an Intuitive Medium and opens her mind to new ideas about life, spirits, and the afterlife.

"New" or "different" triggers curiosity. At the same time, if you were walking through the jungle a few hundred thousand years ago, "new" could also be dangerous if you wanted to try a never-seen-before poisonous berry.

Growth mindsets can be a mixed bag.

You may have a friend who loves to travel to new places off the beaten track. At the same time we all know the stories of adventurers who travelled to dangerous places and found themselves in trouble.

Doctors are always studying new technologies to solve old problems. Not all of them will work. Sometimes the old tried-and-true is most effective.

You have a growth mindset if you're reading this book and open to new ideas in spirituality, psychology, and science - even if your best friend thinks it's all "hocus-pocus." Maybe she's right, more importantly, maybe she's wrong.

Fixed and growth mindsets vary. You can have a fixed mindset on religion and science and a growth mindset on business and technology. As with most things in life, mindsets can change and be flexible. You use them when it applies.

I call that a *hybrid* mindset.

A Fly-on-the-wall

There was a committee meeting about the next annual block party on a local street. A fly-on-the-wall heard everything in the noisy, sometime combative meeting. Here's what happened.

A year ago, the block party organizers put together a very successful event. Everything went well and people were happy with the results. They wanted to keep it the same.

A group of neighbors disagreed. They had been to the party and recently moved into new homes on the block. "We have face painters and magicians available," they argued. "There are local teen bands that will be thrilled to participate for free. They'll bring in a lot more people and make it *better* than last year."

Last year's organizers shook their heads. "Everyone had a great time last year. Why change?"

Why not change?

Who's right?

Fixed mindsets would keep it the same. Growth mindsets would want to try something new – even if it might not work.

What would you choose?

Why are mindsets so important?

Mahatma Gandhi, who used nonviolence to lead India to independence, inspiring civil rights movements around the world, advised, "Live as if you were to die tomorrow. Learn as if you were to live forever."

Mindsets frame your life. They might guide you on how to think and what to try – support your willingness (or unwillingness) to test new ideas with only a "feeling" that they'll work. They might inspire you to take risks and go outside the box.

Most people like to think they have growth mindsets. That's not always the case. You're probably very comfortable in many established attitudes and behaviors. Maybe they come from your childhood, ethnic group, religion, or community. You don't *want* to give them up.

Ask yourself this: do you want to convert to another religion (even if you're not religious)? Why become a runner when you always walked? Why cook chicken soup in the microwave when your grandma taught you to make it on the stovetop?

Mindsets define who you are, what you believe, how you choose your partner, raise your kids, and how you learn. If your mindset is fixed, you avoid challenges. You don't "learn as if you were to live forever." Instead, you believe that your abilities, intelligence, and creativity are fixed from birth.

A growth mindset is open – you're always learning and embracing change. The outcome may be positive if you give it a chance. If it doesn't work there's always another way.

I think of a mindset like a very tall fence. It may block what you can see, hear, and experience. Climbing over that fence is risky; you can't be sure of what you'll find. *Not* climbing over the fence might be a missed opportunity.

Then there's going beyond your mindset where Paranormal Is My Normal. I can take you to a place beyond your physical senses.

Ask yourself this:

If a tree falls in the forest and there's no one to see or hear it, does it make a sound?

If it's a sunny afternoon with a clear blue sky does that mean there are no stars or planets past the clouds?

If there's a life form, deep in the ocean, that no human has seen, photographed, or named does that means it doesn't exist?

Science as a Mindset.

Dr. Eben Alexander, author, neurosurgeon, and neuroscientist, wrote in *Proof of Heaven*, "we are not prisoners in this world, but voyagers through it."

What did he mean? Let's take a look at his story.

Alexander was a highly respected neurosurgeon with a fixed science mindset. One morning he woke up with severe back pain. Nothing could make it better. The pain got worse and he was rushed to the hospital. The diagnosis was deadly - acute bacterial meningoencephalitis – a brain infection that 90% of people couldn't survive.

He fell into a deep coma, totally unresponsive. His family was told that they would lose him within days.

Later, Alexander would write, "My coma taught me many things. First and foremost, near-death experiences, and related mystical states of awareness, reveal crucial truths about the nature of existence."

While "unconscious," Alexander saw a different place, filled with white light, incredible beauty, and a feeling of being "ultrareal."

After seven days, Alexander came out of the coma, a different man. He felt enlightened, believing he discovered that life exists after death. He now tells his story over and over in books, speeches, interviews, and on the internet. He wants everyone – including the scientific mindsets – to understand the nature of the reality he experienced.

How did scientists respond? Most of them didn't believe Alexander's story.

Today's world is grounded in a science mindset that can be fixed, growth, or hybrid. Ideas, proof, statistics, and the ability to measure observations is key. For example, your favorite basketball player has to have good statistics to be the best. You know you have the flu if you test positive. Some people argue that there's no God because we cannot measure or prove a divine existence. Other people take the opposite view and refuse the idea of evolution, claiming the biblical belief that the world was created in seven days.

Consider another story. A lot of healthy people suddenly got sick with a strange pneumonia-like illness. First scientists searched for a common bacteria in the sick people. Next they looked for places where those people might have been exposed to the bacteria. The scientists discovered that the sick people were in hotels, cruises ships, and places with cooling systems. They tested those places to see if the bacterial was there.

That's how scientists discovered Legionnaires' disease!

Clearly, the scientific mindset led to a diagnosis and cause. It worked. We needed it.

Now consider some very famous people who moved beyond the scientific mindset of their times.

Copernicus, Renaissance mathematician, physician, and astronomer, bucked a 16th century belief that the sun, not the Earth, was the center of the universe.

Sir Isaac Newton identified gravity when, as legend tells us, he saw an apple fall to the ground.

Alexander Graham Bell, inventor and teacher of the deaf, had the crazy notion that voices could travel large distances, unseen. He invented the first practical telephone. Ironically, both his mother and wife were deaf.

Copernicus couldn't *see* planets rotating around the sun, Newton could only *feel* gravity, and Bell spent much of his time talking to people who couldn't hear.

Powerful, creative scientists go way beyond what's visible to our senses to understand the world.

What if *you* can't see something? What if your words, tools, and technology can't measure it scientifically? Does that mean it doesn't exist? Does that mean the tree made no sound, the sky has no stars, or the never-seen-before life form isn't there?

Of course not. Copernicus, Newton, and Bell, all went outside the scientific mindset of their time. They knew that something was beyond. Scientists make discoveries in the universe not always by seeing them directly but reactions to other objects in space.

They are also going beyond their scientific mindsets.

We need both – the scientists who discovered Legionnaire's Disease and pioneers who took a risk on things they couldn't see.

Leonardo da Vinci

Most people think of Leonardo DaVinci as the artist who painted the *Mona Lisa.* He was so much more, living beyond the mindsets of his time in art, architecture, and science.

DaVinci (1452-1519) epitomized the term, "Renaissance Man." He is best known for his art but many people overlook his dozens of secret notebooks filled with inventions, observations, and theories from anatomy to aeronautics. He was way ahead of his time, creating (on paper) inventions like the bicycle, the helicopter, the airplane, and the submarine – centuries before any of these things became realities. He studied human anatomy and in 1490 drew the famous *Vitruvian Man* or "The proportions of the human body according to Vitruvius."

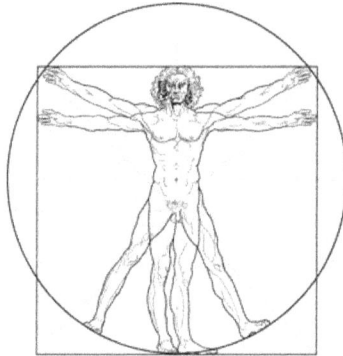

3   BEYOND MINDSETS

The Mediums' Book, 1861

By Allan Kardec

"If the belief in spirits and in their manifestations were an isolated exception . . . it might, with some show of reason, be attributed to illusion; but how is it that we find this belief in vigor among all peoples, ancient and modern, as well as in the writings recognized as sacred in all known religions?

Prove to us that the existence of spirits, and their manifestations, are contrary to the laws of nature; prove they are not, and cannot be, a result of natural law."

I've dealt with many different mindsets in my work. They complement one of the most amazing functions of the human brain – the ability to adapt and change from experience.

When you change your mindset, become open to new ideas and experiences, your brain actually rewires itself. Brain cells respond to new energies, reorganizing, restructuring, and building new connections. How does it work and more importantly, what does it mean?

Think about changing your job. Suddenly you're in a different environment or industry and have to learn everything new. There's new people, technology, and systems. You may have a new commute – even a different dress code. Everything shifts in big and little ways. You change and adapt to make a better life for yourself. Your brain rewires itself.

Maybe you're moving to a different city or state. From an apartment to a house? Whether it's five miles or five thousand miles, everything is different in a new neighborhood. You have to get used to new street names and stores. Everything is unfamiliar.

In the beginning you might feel awkward, even homesick. Slowly you learn the new customs, meet new people, and change your behavior. The next time you put on a coat because it's too cold or take it off because it's too warm, you can appreciate the fundamental human capacity to adapt.

Let's move beyond. Instead of feeling the warmth or coldness of a place, imagine being in a space where you feel rather than see; where energy and light dominate; and proof is in experience rather than measurable facts.

That's where I do my work.

Since the dawn of human civilization, people have called this *paranormal.* Paranormal describes experiences beyond normal scientific understanding. It doesn't mean something is non-existent only that our present tools, technology, and science can't see it, measure it, or prove it, *yet.*

When I saw my first spirit at age six, I just assumed everyone saw and heard the same things. It wasn't scary or upsetting. That was the way I experienced my world.

Some kids have invisible friends; others have superhero fantasies. Some kids believe they can become famous Hollywood Stars. I believed I could become a famous basketball player.

What feels more paranormal than an Emperor marching without clothes; a fairy protecting Peter Pan; or little green leprechauns guarding a pot of gold at the end of the rainbow? Children believe there are seven dwarfs and unicorns that fly. They don't worry about whether it is or isn't normal.

The older we get the more we think about the paranormal. We are fascinated by stories about haunted houses and movies about Angels. These spiritual beings are said to exist in places often called by different names like Heaven or Paradise.

Studies have shown that nearly 72% or roughly 3 out of every 4 people believe there's a place you go after death.

The paranormal is part of who we are – even if we fear or ridicule it.

I believe there are other dimensions - spaces where spirits, angels, masters, guides, and human consciousness thrive. There are also dimensions that have no physical definition, time, or space in Earthly terms. I know it's there because I've seen and heard it. It's filled with light and energy beyond our Earth-bound senses. Beauty, peace, and love are everywhere.

I call it *Inside the Light*.

Famous Paranormal Phenomenon

*The ancient Greek philosophers believed that the "soul" departed the body at death, headed for a nonphysical space.

*Mark Twain was a member of the *English Society for Psychical Research,* trying to understand the role of spirits in his life.

*Winston Churchill slept in the Lincoln bedroom in The White House during World War II. Churchill had just finished his bath and was still naked when he reportedly saw Lincoln's ghost. The story claims that the two looked at each other and Churchill commented, "Good evening, Mr. President. You seem to have me at a disadvantage."

*Michel Nostradamus, a 16th century French physician, astrologer, and seer, correctly predicted many tragic events in future history including the defeat of Napoleon, the rise of Hitler, and the 9-11 terrorist acts. His predictions are subject to interpretation.

*Abraham Lincoln and his wife, First Lady Mary Todd, supposedly held séances in the White House to contact their dead son, Willie.

*According to history.com, the most famous haunted house is The White House, where Presidents, First Ladies, Staff, and guests have reported ghosts, unexplained noises, and strange apparitions.

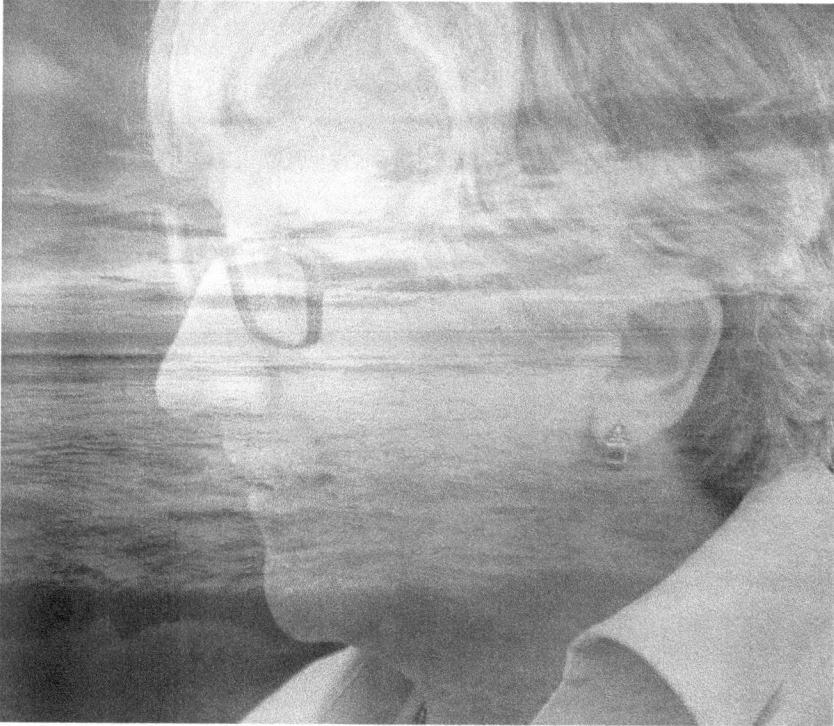

4 INSIDE THE LIGHT

Inside the Light is bigger than we can imagine – so complex that it challenges all our mindsets. It's difficult to describe when words and pictures can only tell a small part of the story.

People have referred to Inside the Light by many names, such as The Other Side, The Astral Plain, and The Hereafter. Some people don't believe it exists; most feel there's something that comes after death where people are eternally rewarded for leading a good life.

Scientists and philosophers have tried to understand Inside the Light. Many say that reality is defined by only what we can see, measure, or prove by scientific observation. Others, equally trained, disagree.

Raymond Moody, physician, psychologist, and philosopher has spent most of his adult life studying human consciousness and life after death. "I have absolutely no fear of death," he says. "From my near-death research and my personal experiences, death is, in my judgment, simply a transition into another kind of reality."

Where and what is that reality? The idea is bigger than we can imagine – a concept almost beyond comprehension. I *know* that it exists Inside the Light.

Skeptics talk about how it's impossible; life ends when it ends; and Inside the Light is a fantasy. Religion tells us there's something after death but usually it's in their terms. They all believe in their God as the *only* God, described in Earthly terms. It doesn't mean they're wrong – in my experience, there's just more to it.

I believe that God is everywhere – in everything we do – and within each of us.

Who is beyond us?

Beings exist in other dimensions, galaxies, and universes. What I see, experience, and write about in this book is just a tiny piece of the many levels of existence.

It's like a grain of sand on an endless beach.

Dr. Michio Kaku, theoretical physicist, futurist, university professor, and innovator beyond traditional scientific mindsets, explains what he believes is happening today. There's a "whole new set of facts" waiting to be discovered. We'll find, with more exploration of outer space, that we're not alone. Our universe is one of many.

It's called a *multiverse*.

Dr. Brian Greene agrees, writing in *The Hidden Reality,* "what we've long thought to be the universe is only one component of a far grander, perhaps far stranger, and mostly hidden reality."

That means there are an endless number of universes beyond our own. There are unlimited realities, dimensions, and energies.

Inside the Light is part of this vast space, filled with light, energy, and spirits. The beings Inside the Light connect with me; I've experienced pure, elegant, graceful beauty that our Earthly eyes can't see. I feel them in my soul. Inside the Light is Divine Space.

I know, without any doubt, that we're not alone.

Can you describe Inside the Light?

Words are limited, technology, in its present state, can't help us.

There's no beginning or end *Inside the Light.* It's more like a sunrise over the ocean. There's peace and quiet; a pure energy that doesn't move but waits for direction. Everything is stable and comforting; form and content hidden within.

Let's explore it in Earthly terms.

When you look at the ocean beach we all see something different. I see waves, whitecaps, and horizon. You might see the light glistening off the waves. A weatherman may see a storm approaching.

We look at the same thing but see it differently.

It's the same with *Inside the Light.*

Inside the light is very quiet and calm. The soul has no Earthly body. Peace dominates, reflecting the continuous movement of the soul through time. There's no judgment or inner critic; only a strong sense of mind reflecting light and human consciousness. Only our imaginations can glimpse at what's out there.

Anita Moorjani, author of *Dying to Be Me,* wrote that her body or physical traits weren't with her while in a coma, "yet my pure essence continued to exist . . . *not* a reduced element of my whole self [but] far greater and more intense and expansive . . . magnificent . . ."

My Visits Inside the Light

No end. No beginning. It's the Alpha and Omega. Everything exists beyond human imagination. There's quiet in the peacefulness, like a soft, unspoken word. I feel a pure, vibrant energy that awaits direction, patient for us to give it form and content.

It feels *alive.*

People who are clothed in light approach. They shimmer in white light. There are souls who incarnated on Earth and those who are waiting for incarnation.

Wide, expansive paths of light welcome me. I can follow one to a crystal structure. This is where the "masters" live (not in Earthly terms). It's pure, divine energy in the shape of spiritual beings who work to help the people on Earth.

The crystal structure holds 12 masters. I've worked with them before. They first showed themselves with Mrs. Ryan when I was 6 years old. They're my circle of spiritual beings who help me in my work and nurture my own soul's growth. They have been with me throughout time, guiding me through everything I've learned on Earth and Inside the Light.

They're way beyond any mindset – a pure, elegant, graceful force that our eyes can't see but our souls can feel. They tell me that no one is ever alone.

Who lives Inside the Light?

There are many different beings who guide us: Spirits, Angels, Masters, Guides, and other entities. Divine energy takes on diverse shapes and forms, traveling through many dimensions.

Spirits are in an energy form. They can come and go when incarnated into the physical dimension we know as Earth. I believe that each of us has done that many times. Spirit forms travel through different dimensions and forms whenever they want.

Angels are the care takers of souls presently alive on Earth. They "bring" back and forth spirits that move through time and space. They also take care of souls Inside the Light.

The Masters exist at a higher level where they direct and advise souls or spirits finding their way into physical Earth. They counsel. The Masters oversee the spirit's journey through time and space, advising souls before and after they're in a physical form.

My 12 Masters guide me from a crystalline structure. They have been with me throughout time. I've seen them since I was a child, helping me to understand my gift, negotiating friends and family who "didn't get me," and empowering me to improve my abilities. They will also correct me if I get too smug or sure of myself.

They're very much a part of this book.

Other spirits watch over communities of souls that come and go throughout time.

We all have a soul group where we're spiritually connected. Whether in spirit or in the physical world, there's a bond among members of a soul group.

I know the idea of a soul group sounds very strange – more like science fiction or fantasy. I'll put it into Earth terms. Ever meet a complete stranger and had the feeling that you knew or met them before (even if you didn't)? Were you ever unusually attracted to someone and had no idea why? Do you have a friend or family member who knows you better than yourself, as if you've been linked for a very long time?

They're probably members of your soul group. Those strange, sometimes intense feelings of connection are your soul's response.

Guides are another type of spirit being who can be in the physical earth without a body. They follow a spirit through their incarnation, giving them cues on the right and wrong way of being. However, each of us *always* has free will and the ability to choose how you want to live a life.

Those are the main beings. I think of them like invisible neighbors who you know are there but you can't see their house.

What is the realm of peace?

The realm of peace is within all of us. It's where you find calm, peace, and a place to heal.

When things don't go as planned, stress takes over. Maybe you lost your job; your best friend betrayed you; or you got stuck in endless traffic. Emotions flare. You can't help it. That's the perfect time to ask these three questions:

Why am I angry?

Why am I irritated?

Why is it bothering me so much?

Stress and negativity triggers emotional, mental, physical, and spiritual responses. They don't feel good; usually increasing anger and pessimism. Instead of confrontation, you have the power to do the opposite – center yourself, find balance, and not allow the negative thought patterns or energy to invade your space.

You can reach into the divine being inside all of us; step into the realm of peace – a healthy, calm, and tranquil space within. In other words, drop into yourself.

I use tools like saying "I am peaceful" or "I am happy" or any words or thoughts to bring me inside, away from the negative triggers outside.

Allow calm and peace *in* you. The realm of peace is where you're totally accepted and unconditionally loved.

The more you enter the realm of peace, the happier you are.

5   CAN ANYONE GO INSIDE THE LIGHT?

We are God and God is us.

We have travelled through time and thousands of incarnations. Ironically, most of us have *forgotten* that we're all divine beings.

We've replaced our memories with our egos and mindsets.

1877-1945

Edgar Cayce directly influenced me since I began my journey. Known as the sleeping prophet, Cayce is credited with hundreds of thousands of pages of information on spirit, health, healing, the soul, and our connection to God Consciousness. Cayce wrote, "The ultimate purpose of our life is to rejoin God in conscious participation of divinity."

We've all lived Inside the Light and continually receive signs from the spirits. We need to listen to our souls and not allow physical rules, ideas, and stressors to block signs from the spirits.

Children are more open to spirits.

Like my experience with Mrs. Ryan, I wasn't scared. It made me feel better and more connected. Unlike my experiences, this child was ridiculed for talking to her departed grandfather. She learned how to close the door.

Visiting with Pop

I was only ten years old when my beloved grandfather, "Pop," passed on after a long battle with liver disease. No one told me very much except that he was gone - dead - and I would never see him again.

I didn't believe them. So I began writing letters every night before I went to sleep. I told him about the things going on in my life and in the family. I wrote how much I missed him. Then I tucked the letters under my mattress where I knew no one would find them. I crawled under the covers and went to sleep, dreaming about Pop smiling and comforting me.

One day I came home from school and found my family laughing at me. "We found your letters," Dad said, pointing to the papers spread on the kitchen table.

I was mortified. I must have done something very wrong. I ran away from their laughter and threw myself on the bed, burying my head in the pillow. I started to cry – the tears made my body tremble.

"I miss you so much, Pop," I said into the pillow.

I never wrote another letter. But in my mind, I still dreamed about, talked to, and visited Pop.

Have I already communicated Inside the Light?

These days, people talk about it more than in the past. Too many find it scary, a bad dream, or a vivid imagination.

They're so wrong!

You *have* communicated with departed loved ones! We all receive messages from spirits who exist Inside the Light. The signs may be subtle or specific – a message that comes in a feeling, impression, image, or dream. When you're ready to listen there might be the scent of a familiar perfume; finding a dime and one penny with a special meaning; or a unusual butterfly hovering by your window. These signs are affirmations that your departed loved ones are with you, watching over you with love.

Below are some common signs from Inside the Light:

*Vivid Dreams

*Spirit signs

*Electrical/Electronic Interference

*Sensing a presence – feeling a departed loved one is "with you"

*Finding feathers in a place where they don't belong (especially white)

*Recurring patterns that don't seem like coincidence

*Something unusual occurs for no real reason

*Images during meditation when our minds are "cleared"

*Unexplained "warm" chills

*A single butterfly

*Physical sensation that someone is touching you (and no one is there)

*Numbers appear that are relevant to you or your departed loved one

*A feeling of unconditional love and overwhelming peace

6   THE NEAR DEATH EXPERIENCE –
A DOORWAY TO INSIDE THE LIGHT?

We have studied twenty thousand cases of people all over the world who had been declared clinically dead and who later returned to life . . . dying is a birth into a different existence.

-Dr. Elisabeth Kubler-Ross, MD, *on LIFE after DEATH*

I was a teenager when I first heard about the Near Death Experience (NDE). It immediately caught my interest. I thought it may be a clue to Inside the Light, so I began to explore.

Most of us have heard about the NDE. People have been talking about it since ancient times, recording it in every racial, ethnic, cultural, economic, and religious group on the planet. A lot of different people and specialists have studied it, including scientists, philosophers, and parapsychologists. There's been a wide range of speculation and theorizing, but no real answers.

Although I've never experienced an NDE myself, I've heard many stories about what happens. The NDE occurs when people face imminent death. It could be from an illness, brain disorder, cardiac arrest . . . even a fatal car accident. The cause of physical death isn't important – only that the brain or heart stops, breathing ends, and the person is believed to be clinically dead.

The Near Death Experience happens when people are brought back to life, usually with technology like CPR (cardiopulmonary resuscitation) or a defibrillator. The person spent time being clinically dead and was resuscitated.

Many of us love medical dramas. It's hard to find one where someone doesn't go into cardiac arrest and the handsome hero doctor dramatically brings them back to life. It's usually a heart-stopping moment on screen until life is restored and the patient smiles. Everyone lives happily ever after the final commercial.

The stories are great but they're mostly fiction.

An interesting study, published in *The New England Journal of Medicine,* "Cardiopulmonary Resuscitation on Television – Miracles and Misinformation" found that 75% of characters who received CPR on TV survived while in real life it was less than 30%.

With that in mind let's look at the people who are brought back to life *and* experienced an NDE.

NDE stories have common elements. Even though they were clinically dead, *something* happened. Something that shouldn't be possible when the body is dead and there's no brain, heart, or breathing and life is technically over.

Some people who were never clinically dead but in a coma report similar Near Death Experiences. Others claim to have experienced NDEs without dying – usually in dreams and meditation.

NDEs happen more than you realize

The IANDS (International Association for Near Death Studies) reports that 4-15% of the population have had an NDE.

Many people hesitate to tell their stories because they're afraid of being embarrassed, laughed at, or considered "weird." When they feel safe and not afraid, NDE survivors are generally eager to share their stories and what many think of as new-found knowledge.

Researchers like Dr. Jeffrey Long have worked hard to understand where a NDE survivor "goes" in the time between life, death, and resuscitation.

Dr. Long studied 1300 people reporting NDEs. He found an odd "consistency in NDEs in organized, lucid experiences at the time when they're clinically dead."

Strange, seemingly impossible visions in an NDE often sound more like the stuff of science fiction or fantasy than reality. They frequently report experiences similar to what I described in my visits to Inside the Light. Most NDE survivors conclude that it's a glimpse into what happens after death.

An NDE often begins with the feeling of being outside the physical body. Others recall an overwhelming sense of calm, comfort, and peace. Some recount conversations they couldn't have heard – like doctors working to resuscitate them or people outside their hospital rooms. This out-of-body experience isn't frightening; there's no pain, fear, or sense of danger. They describe an odd separation of consciousness as if they're all there but in a different form than the physical body.

Nearly everyone sees a light at the end of a tunnel or the other side of a gate.

They move toward the light. As they get closer, many see loved ones who have passed, religious spirits, angels, and friends. They're in a heaven-like place filled with intense feelings of joy and peace. The "world" is light, energy, and unconditional love.

A few speak of life review without judgment, filled with acceptance and unconditional love. It's similar to what is popularly known as life "flashing before your eyes."

In this dreamlike NDE state, perceptions, thoughts, feelings, and consciousness remain intact. They think, hear, feel, and speak the same, communicating by telepathy. Eventually a "border" appears – or choice – to decide whether to remain Inside the Light. Often there's help in making the decision - perhaps a loved one or angel reminds them that it's not time - there's still too much to be done on Earth. Many NDE survivors say that they don't want to go back to their physical body and try to remain where they are

NDEs have been described in books, interviews, videos, movies, television, even *You Tube*. Some of them are regular people like you meet on the street or live next door, others are scientists and physicians. Everyone has an opinion.

There are subtle changes in NDE survivors, like what Dr. Elisabeth Kubler-Ross described in her book, *The Cocoon & the Butterfly.* The image of a butterfly emerging from a cocoon is a symbol of a new and beautiful beginning. Similarly, after an NDE, an individual tends to shift how she or he views life.

Most are happier, more at peace with their lives, and no longer afraid of death.

They have a greater appreciation of life, better self-esteem, greater compassion for others, and deeper spirituality. Some report a heightened sense of intuition and the need to help others.

No one knows *why*.

Paul's Story

"It happened to me," Paul said. His eyes widened, and his face filled with awe. "I was on the table and my heart failed. I could hear the doctors and the machines trying to bring me back. I could see their faces and understand their words." He sighed.

"I floated out of my body and over my hospital bed. All of a sudden I was in a dark tunnel. I wasn't scared. There was a bright light at the end. It was peaceful, warm, and comforting. I felt, rather than saw, people around me, gentle and loving. The pain was gone. It was if they were all there for me."

He smiled softly. "I moved toward a bright light and found myself deeper in the tunnel. I wasn't scared - just happy to be there. Then I heard my mother's voice as if she had talked to me that morning.

It's not your time.

I didn't want to go back, but she spoke again, not words but in my head.

It's not your time.

"No. I want to stay."

It was so peaceful – full of joy. It *felt* good. Why would I want to go back? But there was no choice. It wasn't my time. I knew it without thinking or saying the words. It wasn't my time. I would be back someday, just not now.

Suddenly I was at the hospital, my heart beating.

"He's back," the doctor said.

Paul looked straight into my eyes. "Don't be afraid of death," he said softly, without any doubt. "It's a beautiful place."

7   THE DEBATE OVER NDE

The debate over NDE is ongoing. There are many ideas and no real concrete proof – except it happens. Is it a peek Inside the Light? No one has any explanations other than it *is*. Too many people have reported the experience today, yesterday, in history, and will probably in the future.

Maybe science and spirituality are different sides of the same coin. It's like looking at the ocean – people see the same scene with different observations and interests. They all count. One day all these ideas will be celebrated for their diversity and their likeness connecting us to a larger picture.

Each one has truth and each one has a missing link yet to be identified by technology, science, or faith.

What do neuroscientists say about NDE?

Neuroscientists and medical mindsets believe the NDE is purely physical. A combination of factors such as low (or no) oxygen, cardiac arrest, brain damage, and changes in blood chemistry can cause the reported "experiences."

They speculate that it's the result of side effects from drugs used during resuscitation; natural chemicals released in the brain; or disturbed blood gases and brain malfunctions

Many claim suggest that the NDE is a hallucination created by a dying brain.

How does that happen in coma, after the heart stops, breathing stops, the brain dies, and the body no longer functions?

Ask Dr. Eben Alexander, neurosurgeon and author, who wrote in *The Map of Heaven,* "For the vast majority of our time on this planet, human beings didn't doubt for a moment that the spiritual was real." He never agreed until after his seven-day coma and NDE experience. Alexander wasn't supposed to survive but he did – totally intact – to completely change his views on life after death.

Keep in mind that science is critical in our lives and continuing understanding of the world. It shouldn't be completely rejected only questioned in the case of NDEs.

What do spiritualists say about NDEs?

As an Intuitive Medium and Healer, I have no doubt there is life after death. Most spiritualists agree that NDEs are proof of the afterlife. I, along with many others, think in terms of the human consciousness or soul. All souls separate from the physical body upon death.

During an NDE the soul travels to Inside the Light.

Spirit guides and other already-passed-on souls may recognize that it's not the right time and prompt the NDE individual back to her or his physical body.

Dr. Kubler-Ross wrote that death is "identical to what happens when the butterfly emerges from its cocoon." The "cocoon" is your physical human body; like a house where you live. "Dying is only moving from one house into a more beautiful one," she added.

The NDE survivors choose to return to life after their peek Inside the Light.

Spirituality is about the human soul, understanding your place on Earth and Inside the Light.

Can they both be right?

I like to believe that spiritualists and neuroscientists are both right. One day we'll discover that they're just different views of the same truths.

The human body has both light energy and physical matter. When it dies, the physical body decays but what happens to the energy?

According to Albert Einstein, "energy cannot be created or destroyed, it can only be changed from one form to another."

There is a part of each human that "lives" in the physical body but doesn't need it to survive. Some call it the soul; others refer to it as human consciousness. Either way, no one has been able to prove its existence - yet we all *know* it's there.

It is the part of you moved by the immensity of the ocean and the endlessness of the universe filled with galaxies, planets and stars. It is that moment when you feel a rush of unconditional love in your heart. It is a cloud formation that becomes an angel right before your eyes. It is the rainbow that brings you peace as you wonder how the sky can bring such beauty into your world.

You are reading this book because your soul is calling out, in need of more understanding of itself, and how it live in the world.

The soul/higher human consciousness makes you who you are.

Many researchers believe that when the physical body dies, photons or light energy emerge. Because of their size and speed, photons can travel in the multiverse and "live" in parallel dimensions.

Each of us "lives" after death, fully intact, in another form - light energy. NDEs are a window into that transformation.

As an Intuitive Medium with expanded consciousness, I can see, exist in, and communicate in these dimensions of light energy.

You can too. It's just more direct with me.

What's real?

Whether you believe in the spiritualist, scientific, or combined view you *know* that the Near Death Experience happens, over and over again, from ancient times to the present. It's a window – a quick view – into what happens after death.

Whether you accept it on faith, medical models, or a combination of theoretical physics and astrophysical theory, NDEs can't be denied.

8 ASKED AND ANSWERED

What is a psychic?

A psychic is a person sensitive to spiritual forces that can't be explained by natural laws. They use extrasensory perception (ESP) or telepathy to identify information hidden from the normal senses, tapping into one level of reality to offer guidance.

What is a medium?

A medium connects to the spirit world and delivers messages from people who have passed on. They communicate directly between those who exist Inside the Light and loved ones on Earth.

What is a healer?

Healers are people who are trained to help people in physical or psychological distress. They're trained in various areas such as reiki, energy medicine, and spiritual healing. They don't necessarily have psychic abilities but are able to open access to healing energies.

What is a channeler?

A person who expresses thoughts or energy from a higher being such as an angel or master. ALL channels are mediums and psychics. A channeler "loans" his or her physical body to the external being.

Can someone be a psychic, medium, healer, and channel all at the same time?

Yes.

It's rare, requiring personal growth, guidance and insights from masters, angels, and higher guides. If you achieve it, you can enter the healing realms where all beings of healing, guidance, and insight help the spirit, body, emotion, and mind.

What is telepathy?

Also called mental telepathy, ESP (extra sensory perception), clairvoyance, and the sixth sense, telepathy is the communication of thoughts, ideas, and beliefs directly from one person's mind to another, without using words or the five physical senses.

Telepathic "voices" are heard in the mind. We're constantly bombarded with telepathic thoughts from our environment that can be chaotic and confusing. Trust voices from yourself, your guides, masters, and angels.

What is meditation?

Meditation, in any form, is concentrated focus to increase awareness to promote relaxation, stress reduction, and spiritual growth.

There are many different types of meditation. The two most popular quiet the thoughts in your mind or guide you on a journey similar to my CD, *Teach Them How to Find Us*. Meditation expands personal growth, quiets the mind, and helps you enter the realm of peace.

What is a soul group?

A soul group is your family of souls who help, guide, and love you as spirits or people in physical form. Soul groups are together in previous incarnations, Inside the Light, and on Earth.

Soul groups are family assigned positions to help the soul and the group evolve. One or many souls might be incarnated in form while others may be Inside the Light watching, guiding, and helping those in their group who have decided to incarnate.

What is a spirit guide?

This is a non-Earth being who aids a living, incarnated human. A spirit guide will direct, protect, inform, and give assistance to people requesting help.

A spirit guide is a soul who has incarnated on Earth plane before and knows the ins and outs of life in physical form. Spirit guides should not be confused with Angels who are assigned at the birth of the soul and will be with them through their whole lifetime.

Where does God fit in?

God is not a person who sits on a throne but a Divine Source that all souls come from. *We are God and God is Us.*

God is in everything and is everywhere. We are part of the God source energy and all of the beings Inside the Light. When we go into physical form we forget our connection to God and lose ourselves in material energy. All souls are directly connected to God.

Are there pets Inside the Light?

Yes. They're with loved ones who have crossed over. Pets connect in a different way than spirits/souls, using visual more than telepathic communication.

Pet Spirits show me pictures of what they did, what special food they liked, their favorite toys, and special places on Earth.

Can you connect with someone who can't speak or speaks another language?

Telepathy is the universal "language" of mental thoughts rather than words.

Telepathy is the way all spirits communicate with me.

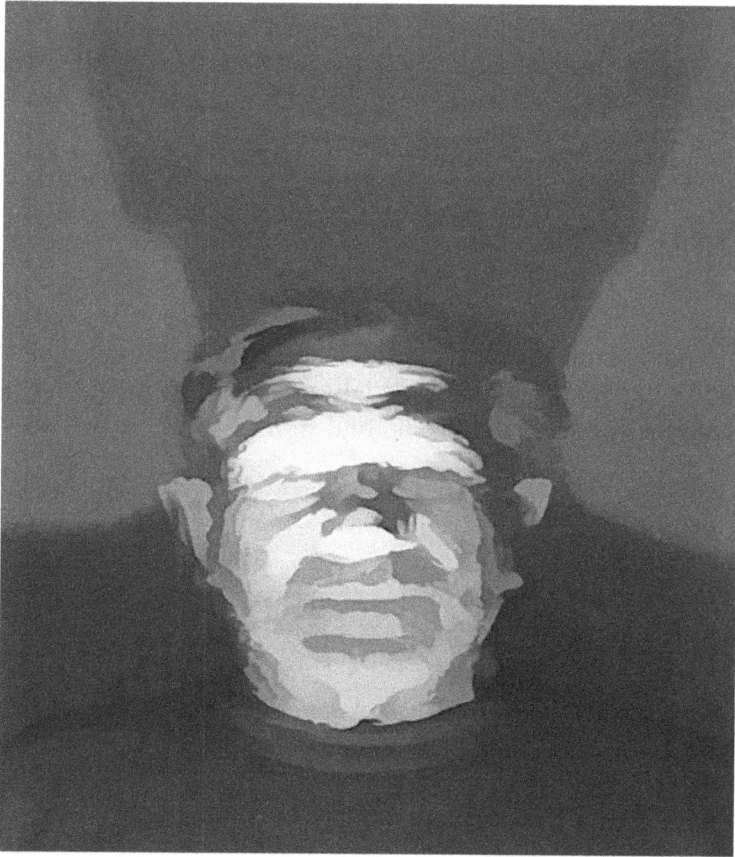

9   PSYCHIC SCAMS

How does a psychic scam work?

Psychic scams come in all shapes and sizes. The one thing they have in common is their goal to make money from innocent people. Some scammers have no psychic abilities. Others have a lot of psychic ability but misuse it to "hook" you. They might tell you there's a dark energy or cloud above you and offer to fix it for a fee. It's an abuse of the psychic ability (for those scammers who have it) or a con game.

When I was in college I knew a woman who went to a psychic and was told she was shrouded in dark energy. For $1200 the psychic promised to take care of it. It took three visits or $3600 before the woman realized what was happening. At that point she stopped but was never able to get her money back.

There are a lot of psychic scam artists. Many telephone and online psychics could be anyone looking to earn extra money. People who are vulnerable, emotionally stressed, or desperate to believe are most easily scammed.

Six ways to spot a psychic scam.

1. Your reading ends with a request for more money, things not done, or items like expensive candles, medallions, amulets, lucky charms, herbs, and potions that seem to have no real significance.

2. You call a psychic or medium hotline and you're told to call back often for information.

3. The "psychic" asks too many questions as if they're fishing for details (they are!).

4. The psychic advertises or makes exaggerated claims like "internationally renowned," 99% accurate, unprecedented.

5. The psychic tries to scare you.

6. You're given false promises or guarantees.

How do you know a Psychic is the real thing?

Psychic ability can be learned but I was born with the ability. I've been with spirits since age six and over the years studied and discovered how to work with integrity. It means I'm somewhat detached, making sure I don't project my personal opinion. It's your life, not mine.

I'm honest, accurate, and specific. I do most of the talking and ask for only necessary, usually affirmative information. Psychic scammers who ask a lot of questions, fumble, give generic answers, or make wild claims are after your money not your spirits. They might also find curses, evil spirits, and darkness, asking for additional money, visits, and purchases that correct the problem.

To make sure a psychic is the real thing, check out credentials, reviews, and "claims." If it looks too good to be true *it is*. Words are cheap, reviews can be made up, and stories may be pure fiction.

On my website, *www.spiritinside.net* I offer testimonials, resources, information about myself and my work. On my Facebook page, facebook.com/realmofpeace, I offer free videochats, commentaries, and suggestions.

Seven important qualities of a psychic who works with integrity

1. They are recommended by someone you trust.

2. Only basic questions are asked – the psychic will look for confirmations.

3. They don't judge or allow personal bias and feelings into the reading.

4. They won't frighten you; if they pick up health issues they might tell you to get something checked out.

5. Honesty is always best.

6. They offer guidance; they never tell you what to do. The choices are always yours.

7. They respect your religious and spiritual beliefs.

Always remember that good psychic work is a calling not a business.

10   TEST YOUR KNOWLEDGE

Read the following questions and circle the best answer. Check it against the answers below.

1. Are we on Earth alone?
    a. Yes
    b. No

2. Which are mindsets?
    a. Fixed
    b. Growth
    c. Hybrid
    d. None of the above
    e. All of the above

3. What are mindsets?
   a. They frame your life
   b. They're the name of a board game
   c. It's a fast food chain

4. What happens when you change your mindset?
   a. You open yourself to new ideas and experiences
   b. Your brain rewires itself
   c. All of the above
   d. None of the above

5. Who are the beings that are always with me spiritually and physically?
   a. Extraterrestrials
   b. My best friends on Earth
   c. Spirit cops
   d. Soul Group
   e. Mediums

6. Do I have a spirit guide?
   a. Yes
   b. No

7. What does paranormal mean?
   a. Crazy neighbors
   b. Experiences beyond traditional or normal life
   c. None of the above

8. Inside the Light has also been called:
   a. The Other Side
   b. The Astral Plane
   c. The Hereafter
   d. All of the above

9. Are there pets Inside the Light?
   a. No
   b. Yes
   c. No rats allowed
   d. No pet crickets allowed

10. What is the language Inside the Light?
    a. English
    b. Chinese
    c. Russian
    d. Telepathy is the universal language understood by all

11. How do you know a psychic scammer?
    a. They ask too many questions or details
    b. They ask for more money
    c. They make guarantees
    d. All of the above

12. Who lives Inside the Light?
    a. Angels
    b. Spirits
    c. Masters
    d. Guides
    e. All of the above

13. What's an NDE?
    a. No dogs enter
    b. New hat emporium
    c. Near Death Experience
    d. Never do exercise

14. What the qualities of a psychic you can trust?
    a. They ask only a few basic questions
    b. They don't have a personal bias in the readings
    c. They respect your religious and spiritual beliefs
    d. They don't scare you with negative and dark energy
    e. All of the above

Answers:

1a, 2e, 3a, 4c, 5d, 6a, 7b, 8d, 9b, 10d, 11d, 12e, 13c, 14e

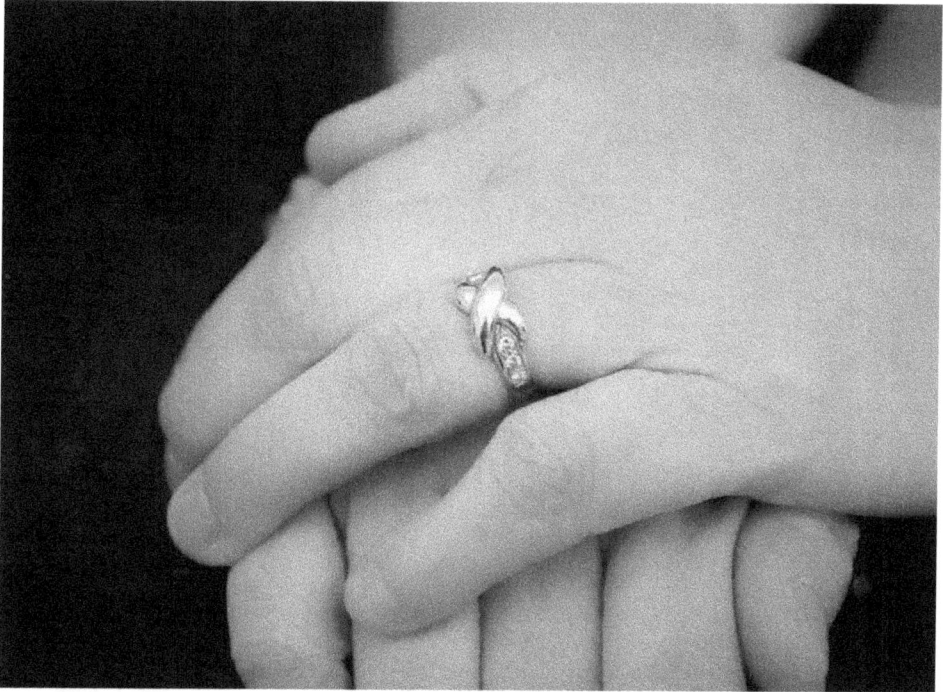

11 JOIN ME

You are in control of your destiny. I can assist you to choose a path of honest and compassionate thoughts and actions. I can guide you into a strong, positive foundation - in business, truthfulness, relationships, and daily life.

You're not alone. There are legions of Angels, Guides and Higher Masters who can and will be able to help. Your good thoughts, loving intentions, and positive affirmations will "signal" these beings. Once these inter-dimensional beings "hear" your thoughts, they'll be able to empower you and help you heal.

Let me guide you.

Here's what I do

Spirit's True Voice - Spirit Connection

I connect with the non-physical world to accurately relay compassionate messages, insights, and higher spiritual perspective. In a spirit connection session I will contact the spirit of your loved one for you.

Through Robin's gentle guidance, I met one of my spirit guides on the beach, who shared with me a beautiful gift of love and support. Receiving my spirit guide's teachings in this way was powerful and had a tremendous and immediate beneficial impact on my well-being and growth. Each day I feel my guide's gift of love and continue to enjoy a dramatic shift in how I approach my life.

Light Board – A Soul's Picture

I use the Light Board to show people how to expand and heal ongoing negative mental and emotional patterns. The goal is to find peace, happiness, and comfort in your daily life. The Light Board is a visual cause and effect of what happens when you align your soul's purpose with your physical life.

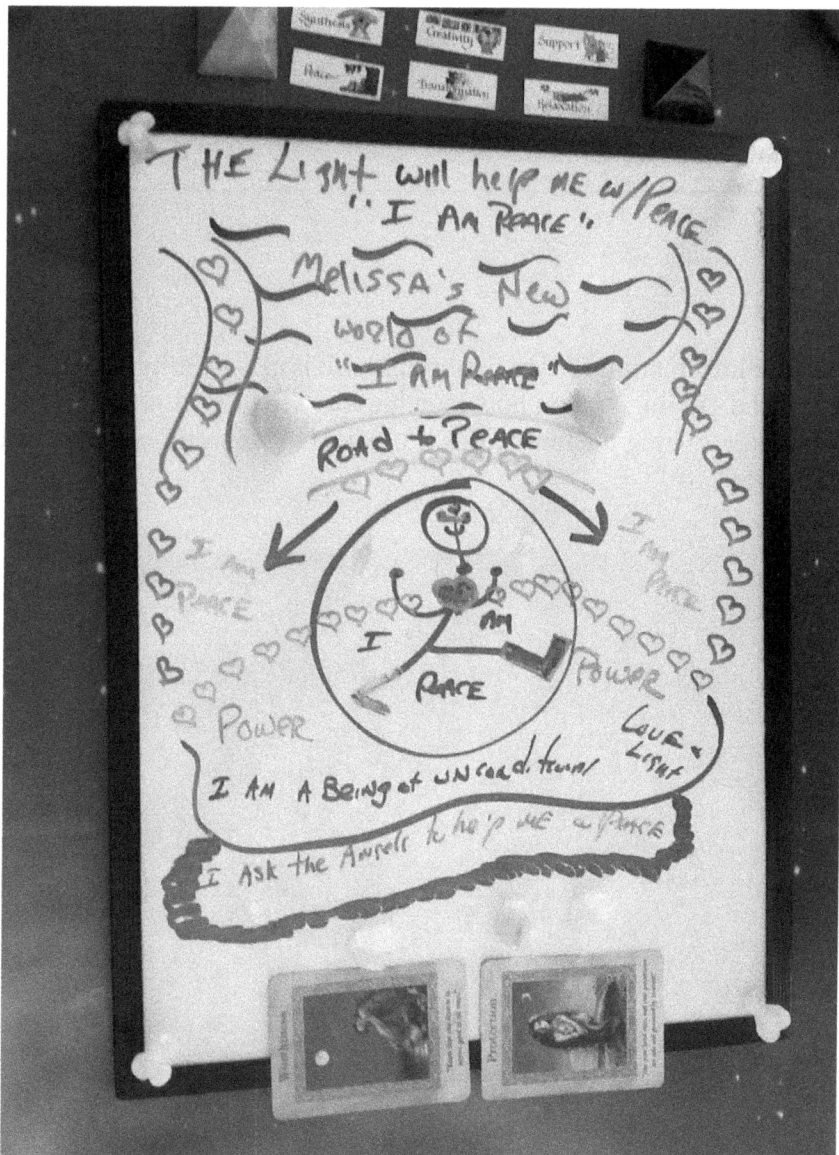

Reiki Hands of Light

In a Reiki Hands of Light Healing session I help you focus on deeper issues to gain a strong understanding of what is holding you back from abundance, joy, health, good solid relationships, and job promotions. I guide you to move gently forward by facing any life challenge.

> I want to thank you so much for our healing session last night. I am so glad that I attended, despite my unfounded anxieties! You always have the wisest and kindest words to share. I experienced so much healing. Your skills as a healer are the best I've ever seen! God could not have chosen a better emissary for His healing work. I feel like a new person - lighter and more empowered.

Beyond Tarot

I access divine information for your everyday life issues by aligning you with your destiny and guiding you on how to achieve a life of health, wealth, happiness and fulfillment. Utilizing the tarot cards, I create a meaningful and clear life path for you to follow.

The Akashic Record Session

I open your soul's records to gain access to information that has been recorded for all your lifetimes. You will be able to ask any questions and connect directly to your soul for guidance and answers needed for assistance on your soul journey. Present day issues, negative, repetitive patterns, emotional pain, mental anxiety, and physical discomfort are all connected to your soul's journey through time. When entering into the Akashic Records you can see your life in a new way, understanding the impact of the past on your present reality.

Here's how I work

Individuals

Small Groups

Community Groups

Workshops

Libraries

Teacher

Lecturer

Fundraiser

Video Chats (on website)

Author

I absolutely LOVED the workshop! Thank you so much for being there for us and helping us do this work. There is nothing like the feeling of knowing we ARE connected, that there is a divine purpose, and our loved ones are much closer than we think! This workshop exceeded all my expectations.

Customized

Create your own customized program! Talk to me and we can work out the best way to maximize you and/or your group experience.

Contact me!

Website: spiritinside.net

Face Book: Robin C. Mueller

Realm of Peace

Email: info@spiritinside.net

Telephone: 914-730-0155

Read more cutting-edge Book Web Minis

Book Web Minis are fun, fast, and hot. Mini books (50-70 pages long) explore up-to-the-minute facts, photos, content, and quizzes to make you the pro. Share with friends, family, and colleagues. Don't wait – get them in eBook or print from Amazon.com.

Bestselling Titles:

Paranormal Is My Normal
SOARING: Seven Steps to Happiness
Timepieces: Yesterday's Stories Today
Photo Power: Hidden Stories
Pocket Cash: Your Way

Bookweb Minis: www.bookwebminis.com

Check out Book Web Fiction

Amazon #1 Bestsellers!

www.hauntedfamilytrees.com

Page turners bursting with haunted family trees, strange lovers, chilling photo insights, and twisted psychopaths burst into life. *Broken Books* reinvent the thriller – blending fact, fiction, and photos into riveting stories you'll never forget. Go to amazon.com to purchase these bestsellers in ebook, print (black & white), and collector's edition (full color print).

Contemporary thrillers:

Broken By Truth (Book 1)

Broken By Birth (Book 2)

Broken By Evil (Book 3)

Don't miss Book Web Historical Fiction

Go back in time to discover how good and evil thrived in the past. Meet the ancestors of the characters in the first three *Broken Books* and follow their legacy.

*Broken By Madness (*Book 4, Dutch New Amsterdam, 1654)

Broken By Men (Book 5, Spain and Portugal, 1490s)

Broken By Kings (Book 6, Sao Tome, Africa, 1494)

Broken: The Prequel (Book 7, Spanish Inquisition, 15th century)

Robin C. Mueller

www.ingramcontent.com/pod-product-compliance
Lightning Source LLC
Chambersburg PA
CBHW081226020426
42331CB00012B/3094